"W

by E. Christina Mayhew

There is still hope, but it will not be easy.

www.whenmillionsvanish.com

2

Preface

Millions of people have just disappeared and you are wondering why. Let me first say that Jesus loves you. Right now the world is in complete chaos. Everyone is terrified and distressed at the same time. If you are reading this book, then you have been left behind while friends or relatives have vanished. I want you to know that they are safe. Aliens did not take them, and other countries do not have "people stealing devices". The news is probably feeding you all kinds or horror stories about what has taken place. The people that have vanished were from all walks of life; every nation is going through the same crisis. You will also see that children under a certain age range are gone because of their innocent state at the time of the event. The people that vanished found a Savior some time ago named Jesus Christ and believed that He died on the cross to save them from their sins. Today, as He promised in the Bible, God has taken them away to Heaven to live with Him. I know some of you don't *want* to believe, *can't* believe or just *won't* believe this, but this is the truth. I am also sure that there are some people still around that honestly thought they knew who Jesus was and find themselves left behind. Think hard about the people that you knew that disappeared. They all had one thing in common: they were *true* Christians; *true* followers of Jesus Christ. This book will tell you how the loving God of Heaven still longs to be with you. It's not too late! You can still go to Heaven. You can still accept Jesus Christ as your Savior. This book will also give you a heads up of what's to come, according to the Bible.

I want all of you to know that there is still hope, but it will not be easy.

"Who is Jesus?" you might be asking. You might even be thinking "I've heard of Him". Let me tell you that He is real. Everything you have ever heard about Him, from the people that have vanished, was the truth. Jesus Christ is the Son of God who died on the cross to pay the debt for our sins. The Bible says in John 3:16: *"For God so loved the world that he gave his only begotten Son, that whosoever believeth in him should not perish, but have everlasting life."* So as you can see, your loved ones did not perish but went to be with the Lord in Heaven. I know many of you have probably heard about Jesus in some way, shape or form. Probably from the people that are not here today. It is not too late for you. On the other hand, there are probably some of you who *have* heard, and have ignored what you heard. You didn't *want* to believe in Jesus. You decided to go about life your own way, doing whatever you chose to do, with no regard for your eternal soul. I'm happy to tell you, even though you were wrong, there is still hope for you! It isn't over and you still can make the right decision.

The Bible says that unless you are "born again" (meaning to accept Jesus Christ as your personal savior), you cannot enter into Heaven. (John 3:3) Again, to be "born again" means to acknowledge that you are a sinner and that Jesus died so you could be pardoned for those sins. Once you have come to that acknowledgment and you have asked Jesus to come into your life as your Lord and Savior, you have just begun a new journey and have entered into the family of God. This is the only way to get into Heaven. If you have just made this decision, I am proud of you. These days are not going to be easy for you, but remember now you belong to Jesus Christ. Even if people harm you, you can have the confidence in knowing that you will be with Jesus one day. Never forget this. Never give in to what's going on in the world around you. Read the Bible to get a better understanding of who Jesus is and His plan for your life. As days go by and you deal with the sorrow of losing someone, not knowing totally what is going on, I ask you to continue to read this book with a Bible close by. I believe that this book will help you. Times are going to change; the world as we knew it will never be the same again. I can only tell you what I believe is going to take place, as the Bible describes and explains it. Honestly, I cannot say that what I am about to tell you will make life any easier, but at least you will be aware of things to come. Please remember that there is still hope! Trust me, there will be times when you will feel hopeless and trapped, but keep in your heart and mind that Jesus Christ is your hope and joy. If you haven't accepted Him, this will be your last chance to find Him.

Chapter 1: Rapture

What you have been witnesses to is commonly referred to in Christian circles as "the Rapture". The word "Rapture" comes from the Latin word "Rapare" which means to take away or to snatch out. The Rapture, as Christians believe, is when God calls home to Heaven those who have served him and believed in him. This belief comes from 1 Thessalonians 4:16-17: *"For the Lord himself shall descend from Heaven with a shout, with the voice of the archangel, and with the trump of God: and the dead in Christ shall rise first: Then we which are alive and remain shall be caught up together with them in the clouds, to meet the Lord in the air: and so shall we ever be with the Lord."*

Some believe that this will take place before God starts pouring out his judgment upon the earth. Some believe that Christians will have to go through certain tests and hardships to prove themselves worthy before God will call them home to Heaven with him. Still, the most common belief is that Christians will be spared, because of the Rapture, from the 7 year period of great hardship known as "The Great Tribulation". (Matthew 24:21)

Nobody really knows at what point in those 7 years God will call those that earnestly followed and loved him home. The Bible says in Mark 13:32 *"that day and that hour knoweth no man"*, but it does tell us to be ready whenever that time comes. Jesus' disciples thought it was going to happen in their lifetime, so they lived as close to His example as possible. They told all who would listen to them the Truth of Jesus Christ and God's promises.

In today's world, the facts are that many Christians have strayed from the truth of God's Word. We're all too busy and caught up with our own lives. We have forgotten that Jesus is coming back one day and that we need to be ready. Just think, if you couldn't stand for Jesus Christ before the Rapture, how in the world will you stand for Him after the Rapture, when people will *certainly* persecute you for your faith? Still, how much harder will it be for those who never had any faith in Jesus Christ to begin with? If either one is you, then I am sorry that nobody ever told you about the love of Christ, or that you rejected what you have heard, but it is not too late. There is hope!

Though this little book is written for those left behind, I ask those who are reading it before the Rapture happens to make sure you are spiritually where you need to be when God calls you home. I believe that some of those left behind will help others find the Lord or re-find Jesus Christ. There's also a chance that Christians will have to go through some of the persecution to come. We just have to know within ourselves who Jesus Christ is and what He has done for us. He gave all that He had for us and deserves our everything.

Chapter 2: Seven Seals – Revelation 6-8

As God starts pouring his wrath out on the earth you are going to see things take place that you never thought possible. In Revelation 5:1 - 6:13, the seven seals are opened, which begins the seven years of The Great Tribulation. The word "tribulation" means great affliction, trial, or distress; suffering. Throughout the Tribulation there will be three segments of God's wrath. The three segments are referred to as the 7 seals, 7 trumpets, and the 7 bowls. We'll touch upon the trumpets and bowls later on in the book.

You are probably wondering why God, if he is so great and merciful, would pour out judgment upon the earth. Why would God do this? God is merciful and great but he is also a just God. God being "just" refers to his character of holiness. God is holy, meaning that he cannot excuse sin. Being just, as in justice, means that he will reward those that follow his holy rules to live by and punish those who don't. He made rules for us to follow because he loves us and wants to keep us safe. He has given us plenty of chances to live life right; by living God's way. Still, it *is* a choice.

You and I know that history doesn't lie and even though people knew about God's holy rules, they still did not live right. For example, if we look back for a brief moment into the Old Testament of the Bible, we see that:

- Adam and Eve sinned by disobeying God. They knew what they had done wrong. God specifically told them not to do something, yet they did it anyway. God didn't destroy them, but punished them for their sin. Because his justice is pure, he had no choice but to punish them. To let them off the hook would have been injustice. (Genesis 3)
- Later, God told Noah to build an ark. People thought Noah was crazy but they all perished in the flood. Those people turned their back on God because the way they were living (in sin) was much more fun to them. God gave them the chance to repent, and they turned it down. Again, God's justice prevailed. (Genesis 6-8)

- God said he would spare Sodom and Gomorrah if there were at least 10 good people living there. Abraham could not even find ten. God's justice demanded that Sodom and Gomorrah be destroyed for their sin. Yet God's mercy allowed him to spare Abraham's brother-in-law Lot because he loved God.
  (Genesis 18-19)

Think about other examples of God's justice throughout history, as you contemplate the chances God has given you in your life and how you responded to them. Were you disobedient like Adam and Eve? Where you Obedient like Noah? Did you ignore God because you were too busy having Godless fun like the people who died in the flood? Did you turn your back on God and curse him like the people of Sodom? Or did you live life the way God wanted you to, despite the evil around you, like Lot? God's judgment is real, but so is his mercy. The 7 seals will very much be like the days of the Old Testament. Be ready.

When the first seal is opened the Antichrist will rise to power. You will not know it is him until he becomes the world leader and brings peace to Israel. Be warned; he has ulterior motives for the things he is doing. You will see peace in the world. This peace will only last a season, yet will yield him great power among the people of earth.

Once the second seal is opened, the peace will end. Most will have been fooled by the Antichrist but now his true colors will start to show. The Bible assures us that as quickly as peace comes, sudden destruction will come as well. This is found in: 1 Thessalonians 5:3 - *"For when they shall say,* **Peace** *and safety; then* **sudden destruction** *cometh upon them…"*

The third seal will be opened and a great famine will hit the earth. This means that people will be starving and dying not only in third-world countries, but everywhere. Think about how much food you could get for a full day's pay. The little food that is available will cost a day's pay for just a day's worth of food. I know we have all seen the commercials about starving people in other countries, but imagine that picture right here in your home town.

Following that the fourth seal will bring even more death to the earth. *"And I looked, and behold a pale horse: and his name that sat on him was Death, and Hell followed with him. And power was given unto them over the fourth part of the earth, to kill with sword, and with hunger, and with death, and with the beasts of the earth."* Revelation 6:8.

People will be killed for their faith as the fifth seal is opened. You will have to choose between Heaven and Hell. Only you can make that choice for yourself. If you die for the cause of Christ you will join the other martyrs that have died throughout history. You will fight by Jesus' side at the end, in the battle of Armageddon.

As the sixth seal is opened the sun will go black and the moon will turn as red as blood. There will be earthquakes greater than anything we have ever seen. Their power will be stronger than any man-made scale can measure. There's been talk of parts of continents some day falling into the ocean because of fault lines and earthquakes. Things like this are going to happen. Many people will be displaced, and will live in caves because there is nowhere else to take shelter. The global landscape will change drastically. Also during this time, keep your eyes and ears open about thousands of people flocking to the country of Jordan.

The seventh seal opens up another set of horrors for the world. God's wrath is not yet satisfied. The knowledge of the sheer magnitude of suffering about to be brought upon the people of Earth causes complete silence in Heaven for a half hour. By the seventh seal being opened, the 7 trumpets are about to sound. Seven trumpets; seven new judgments.

I know this all sounds crazy. Some of you might even be thinking "So what, bad things happen in the world all the time. It's nothing new." You are partly correct about that. Disasters around the world *do* happen all the time, but these new disasters are like nothing the world has *ever* seen. I hope nobody thinks that I am making light of all the terrible situations that have already happened in history; because I am not. I am just trying to make you think of some of the horrible things that have taken place in the world and prepare you for things to come. Imagine what it would be like if the famine, death, war, violence, earthquakes and other natural disasters that we *do* see were all 100 times worse.

This time period is going to be even more perilous and devastating than we could ever imagine. As I mentioned earlier, watch out for the man that brings peace to Israel. He is more dangerous than any of the aforementioned catastrophes.

Chapter 3: Antichrist

The "Antichrist" or "Beast" will be the person to bring peace to Israel and the Middle-East (Daniel 9:27). All people will look up to him as a world leader; even *the* world leader. Leaders around the globe will put their full trust and confidence in him. Soon he will exploit that trust to its fullest potential, thrusting him into a position of world leadership and control. You might be thinking *that* concept is insane and there will never be a "one-world-leader" or a "one-world-religion". You are mistaken. Think about it; if millions vanish all over the world, different countries and religious beliefs will put their differences aside and come together to try to figure out what happened. The Antichrist will lead that charge.

He will fool Jews and Gentiles alike. Performing miracles, he will even bring people back to life. Many will be amazed and therefore mislead. Some will even think that he is the Jewish messiah, foretold in the Bible's Old Testament. He will also have a false prophet by his side, which will truly make people believe that he is who he says he is. Many will believe, I ask you to question everything by what the bible says. God tells us to do that, you have to know who Jesus is for yourself not by what others tell you.

Beware; the Middle-East peace agreement will last for only a short while (three and a half years) and then he will destroy the peace, and reveal his true nature. He will then declare himself to be God. (2 Thess. 2:4)

Now for the "scary" part; in addition to declaring himself to be God, the Antichrist will be empowered by Satan himself. Yes, that means for the next three and a half years the devil literally will be in control of the entire world, only in human form (Revelation 13:2-3). He will do everything in his power to destroy God's remaining people. Remember, even if you perish because of your faith in Jesus Christ, you will be with Him soon and everything will be perfect. The Antichrist cannot stop the wrath that God is pouring out on the earth. If he is claiming to be God, then why is he not stopping the horrible disasters that are devastating the world?

Chapter 4: Trumpets Rev. 8

When the seventh seal has been opened, the second wave of God's wrath will be sounded upon the earth. These things are to come as each trumpet is sounded. Keep your eyes open and continue to trust your faith in Jesus and He will bring you through.

The first trumpet will sound and one-third of the earth will be burned up by great fires and hail storms. We are talking about a land mass the size of Asia being destroyed by fire. This will cause a serious ecological problem. Not only will plants and crops be destroyed, but homes and people as well.

Next, the 2nd trumpet will sound. With this trumpet, one-third of the seas will be turned into blood. Meaning one-third of the living creatures in the sea will die and ships will be destroyed. Food that was once in overabundance in the oceans of the world will be hard to come by in most places.

Following the 2nd trumpet, the third trumpet will sound. A meteor called "Wormwood" will collide with the earth and cause all of our natural drinking water to turn bitter and thus undrinkable. Today we think we have a problem when we have to boil water sometimes when we go camping. After this takes place, that will be the only way you will ever be able to drink water.

Once Wormwood has hit, the fourth trumpet will sound and the lights will go dim. I'm not talking about your electricity, if you even have that anymore. I am talking about the moon, stars and sun. They will lose 1/3 of their natural light. Even the middle of a sunny day will seem like dusk.

Darkness may not seem so bad, but when the fifth trumpet is blown Locusts that act like scorpions will be let lose on the earth. If there's no source of light, you can't see them coming. You'll hear them though. They won't kill anyone but will torture those who are not marked by God. This torture will be so great that people are going to wish they were dead but they won't be able to die. Notice I said those sealed by God would not be harmed. Hopefully by this time you are one of those marked by God.

Those that wish they could die while they are being tortured may soon receive what they hope for. When the 6th trumpet sounds, one-third of mankind will be killed by fire, smoke and sulfur. It is possible that this could be a massive volcanic eruption of some sort. We are talking about around over a billion people.

To end this portion of God's wrath, the 7th trumpet is blown to usher in the beast, or as we have already mentioned, the Antichrist. Earlier we talked about seeing his true colors. Well, you are about to see them as he begins implementing the "Mark of the Beast". He will also condemn all who believe in Jesus Christ. Listen for the two witnesses and be-careful; there will be very few places to hide if any.

Chapter 5: Two Witnesses

Revelation 11:3-6; *"And I will give power unto my two witnesses, and they shall prophesy a thousand two hundred and threescore days, clothed in sackcloth. These are the two olive trees, and the two candlesticks standing before the God of the earth. And if any man will hurt them, fire proceedeth out of their mouth, and devoureth their enemies: and if any man will hurt them, he must in this manner be killed. These have power to shut heaven, that it rain not in the days of their prophecy: and have power over waters to turn them to blood, and to smite the earth with all plagues, as often as they will."*

Two men will appear in Israel during these hard days and will prophesy the truth of Jesus Christ. The two men will prophesy for 1,260 days. What they say will anger many, yet if anyone tries to harm them, fire will come from their mouths and destroy their aggressor. It will not rain during the time they are prophesying. They also will be able to call down plagues from Heaven at will. Once they complete the mission that God has sent them for, and spoken the words that the world needed to hear, the Antichrist will finally be able to have them killed. Their bodies will lie in the streets of Israel for all to see what happens when you oppose and slander the Antichrist. All this is confirmed in Revelation 11:7-10: *"And when they shall have finished their testimony, the beast that ascendeth out of the bottomless pit shall make war against them, and shall overcome them, and kill them. And their dead bodies shall lie in the street of the great city, which spiritually is called Sodom and Egypt, where also our Lord was crucified. And they of the people and kindreds and tongues and nations shall see their dead bodies three days and an half, and shall not suffer their dead bodies to be put in graves. And they that dwell upon the earth shall rejoice over them, and make merry, and shall send gifts one to another; because these two prophets tormented them that dwelt on the earth."*

After three and a half days, they will stand up and fly up into the sky. Yes, I know it sounds crazy, but they will come back to life after three and a half days and then go to be with Jesus. As this happens there will be an earthquake there that will kill 7,000 people. I honestly don't know if the news is going to tell you any of these things, but keep your eyes and ears open. I would suspect that you will hear something about this. Even if you don't see it on the news, you can read about it in Revelation 11:11-13: *"And after three days and an half the spirit of life from God entered into them, and they stood upon their feet; and great fear fell upon them which saw them. And they heard a great voice from heaven saying unto them, Come up hither. And they ascended up to heaven in a cloud; and their enemies beheld them. And the same hour was there a great earthquake, and the tenth part of the city fell, and in the earthquake were slain of men seven thousand: and the remnant were affrighted, and gave glory to the God of heaven."*

Chapter 6: Mark of the Beast

The Mark of the Beast - This is the term in the Bible for the device implanted or tattooed on each person's right hand or forehead which will allow you to buy and sell goods and services, much like a permanent credit card. You will not be able to buy or sell anything without this "Mark". It will be forced upon the people of the world by the Antichrist. The Bible says in Revelation 13:16-17: *"And he causeth all, both small and great, rich and poor, free and bond, to receive a mark in their right hand, or in their foreheads: And that no man might buy or sell, save he that had the mark, or the name of the beast, or the number of his name."* That number will be a mathematic equation equal to 666.

The "mark" will be a piece of financial and personal security technology that will wipe out identity theft and other problems seen by financial institutions. It will contain everything about you; all of your account numbers and personal data. You'll never need to carry a wallet or purse again. They'll be no such thing as cash anymore. It sounds convenient, but in order to get this mark you will eventually have to deny Jesus Christ as the Savior of mankind and the Son of God. The choice will be to take the mark or die, most likely by beheading. It sounds crazy, but the Bible references that part too in Revelation 20:4: *"...and I saw the souls of them that were beheaded for the witness of Jesus, and for the word of God, and which had not worshipped the beast, neither his image, neither had received his mark upon their foreheads, or in their hands..."*

Once the mark is taken, your fate is sealed for eternity. You no longer have any hope of ever seeing your loved ones and friends that vanished. By taking the mark, you denied the only person that could get you to where they are, Jesus Christ. Do NOT take the mark, or whatever the world calls it. You may be put to death, but if you believe in Jesus Christ, a glorious eternity awaits you. Do not be afraid.

One Biblical example of how God deals with persecution of those who are faithful to him is the story of Shadrach, Meshach and Abednego (Daniel 3). Basically the king made an image of himself for the people to bow down to and worship. These 3 young men would not do that because they only worshiped their God. The king had them thrown into a fiery furnace and, wouldn't you know, nothing happened to them! Not one hair on their heads was burned. God put his hand of protection on them because they would not bow to a false god. In these days to come, your faith will be tested like those three Hebrew boys. Yes, you might end up dying for your faith. The Bible also says in 2 Corinthians 5:8 - *"We are confident, I say, and willing rather to be absent from the body, and to be present with the Lord."* This is your hope in the days to come; that if you hold onto your faith in Jesus Christ, and do perish, you will be with Him.

Chapter 7: Seven Bowls - Plagues last of God's Judgment

Rev. 16

You will start to see people who have made the decision to follow the Anti-Christ, who is Satan, or have been put to death because they would not deny Christ. Some of you who have read this book or are reading this book may still be around and still be in hiding. Here is a picture of the next and last part of God's wrath upon the earth.

Watch for these signs, in case you are still out there hidden away and people are trying to find you. Keep an eye out for friends who have taken the mark. There could be people who have taken the mark, and if you haven't, trying to trap you. Once the 1st bowl of God's judgment is poured out, those that have taken the mark will begin to develop boils all over their bodies.

When the second bowl is poured out, the oceans and seas will turn completely to blood. (This is the remaining two-thirds, after Trumpet #2) All living creatures in the oceans and seas will die. There will be no more food coming from them. Many will starve without food brought in by fishermen.

Next, the third bowl will be poured out into the rivers and springs of the world. They too will turn to blood. Forget about boiling the water to drink it; nothing will help. No person or animal will be able to drink from them.

Once the fourth bowl is poured out, you will wish you could swim in the oceans, seas and rivers. The sun will be so hot that it will scorch everyone and every place on Earth. There will be no escaping its blistering heat. Today we can go swimming in our pools, turn on the air conditioning, open the refrigerator and pull out a nice cold beverage. These things may not be there for us to use, and will not help even if they are.

The Antichrist's kingdom will be plunged into complete darkness as the fifth bowl is poured out upon the earth. So now, on top of the boils and sunburns and thirst, they won't be able to see anything. Yet, people will still not turn to God. The Bible says in Revelation 16:10-11 – "*And the fifth angel poured out his vial upon the seat of the beast; and his kingdom was full of darkness; and they gnawed their*

tongues for pain, and blasphemed the God of heaven because of their pains and their sores, and
repented not of their deeds."

It's amazing that even after all of this, people will not admit that they were wrong. Some may see that they made a great mistake, but if they have already taken the mark of the beast, there is no going back. It is already too late for them.

Next, the sixth bowl will be poured out. This will dry up the Euphrates River. If you are still out there at this point- God's judgment upon the earth is almost over.

Finally, once the seventh bowl is poured out, God's judgment on the earth will be over. I know this has not been an easy time by any means but this is the last of it. There will be lightning and thunder storms, severe earth quakes like nothing you have ever seen one-hundred-pound hailstones will be falling out of the sky and crushing people. This will be the end, and will lead to the battle of Armageddon; the last battle between good and evil.

Chapter 8: Armageddon

Armageddon is near the city of Megiddo (southwest of the modern port of Haifa). This will be the place where the last battle will be fought. This battle will be between Jesus Christ, and all who believed in Him, versus Satan, and all the people who followed him and who denied God by taking the mark of the beast. Satan thinks he can win but the Bible is very clear on the matter that the battle has already been won. Satan and his army will be defeated and thrown into the lake of fire never to rise his ugly evil head up again.

You will either be going to heaven with Jesus or you will be thrown into the lake of fire for all eternity. Imagine knowing the truth of Jesus and never ever being able to see Him or make it right.

People laugh and joke about Hell and how great it will be; just one big party. Not quite. Imagine the worst thing that has ever happened to you in this life. Picture it in your head. Now imagine re-living that day, everyday for eternity, never being able to change it in anyway. Hell will be a thousand times worse than that. There's nothing worse than to know what is going to happen, but not being able to do anything about it. I hope you see in this book the things that are going to happen and I pray that you make the right decision so you will one day be with Jesus.

Epilogue

God can handle anything and everything. But imagine the pain and grief of knowing that you gave all you had for someone and they still rejected you. I wrote this book believing in God's grace and mercy and knowing that none should perish without knowing Him. This book wasn't written as justification for people to live their lives however they want and still have one more chance. It was written for those who know the truth (or knew the truth) but something happened in their lives and they strayed from the truth, thus they missed the rapture. You don't want to put off salvation and risk missing the rapture, or worse; dying in your sin. You want to live for Jesus today so you make it to Heaven. No one knows what we will have to go through before the trumpet sounds, so we need to be ready every day as if it is going to be that last day.

If God told you today that the rapture was going to happen tomorrow, how would you spend your last hours here on earth? What would you do, who would you tell? Would you be ready for eternity?

While writing this book, I sent out an e-mail to some of my closest Christian friends. It read: *"I was wondering if I can get your feelings on something. I would like you to think of one person that, if the rapture happened today, you would want to leave a letter behind for them. I don't need the person's name, but I would like to see what types of letters would be left"*. The following are some of the responses I received in reply to that e-mail. I hope these few letters will continue to encourage you as the days go by; knowing that you are loved and cared about. May Jesus Christ be your guide through this period of time.

LETTERS TO THOSE WHO REMAIN

Letter 1:

Dear Loved One,

By now you know that we are no longer together. It was just as we talked about. It was just as the Bible said it would be. All of a sudden, Jesus came through the clouds and took all of his children that asked Jesus to come into our hearts. He took only those of us that truly meant it. By now, you also know that you made the wrong decision, and that is sad.

The good news today is that there's one more opportunity for you. It's going to be harder because you will have to make this decision to follow the Lord and not be able to compromise or negotiate. You see where compromise, negotiation and question have got you? This decision could cost you your earthly life but you will gain from an eternity with Jesus. Let's focus on the future and you have one more chance to make things right with the Lord. Please don't make the wrong decision. This is your eternity we're talking about!!! It's truly beautiful where I am and God wants your heart. Your eternal soul is at stake and you don't have the time anymore to decide. Is it going to be Jesus or Satan? Is it going to be Heaven or hell?

I know you would make the right decision! Please repeat this prayer, and no matter what comes your way…don't turn back or don't waiver your Christianity. Dedicate your WHOLE HEART and your WHOLE SOUL to JESUS.

Dear Jesus

I am a sinner

But I know that I need you

Please come into my heart

Change me

Renew me

Forgive me

And I promise to serve YOU all the days of my life and eternal life

Accept me Jesus

I love you Forever

In Jesus' Name

Amen and Amen

My friend, **YOU ARE NOW A NEW CREATION**. "Therefore, if anyone is in Christ, he is a new creation; the old has gone, the new has come!" 2 Corinthians 5:17

So DON'T TURN BACK and keep looking UP, and soon I'll see you here in a little while.

I love you forever,

Kathy

Letter2:

If I had to leave a letter behind to one person only, that would be very difficult for me. There are many people in my life who are not saved and it is going to break my heart come the day of the rapture when they don't go to heaven with me. I used to think that my mom would be one of those people but God is on the move right now and she was saved a week and a half ago. I think the person that I would want to leave a letter behind to the most would be myself. I know that sounds odd, but it's true. I am not saying that I am not a Christian because I am but what I am saying is that I have made so many mistakes in my past and I am sure I would make some more in my future that I honestly can say that I am not sure if I am guaranteed a spot in Heaven right now. I am struggling with so many things that sometimes I forget what is most important to me and that is Christ. If getting into heaven is based on belief alone, then yes, I would go up in the rapture but there is so much more to serving God then just believing. Choosing to be a Christian is a life style, you can't have the best of both worlds and over the course of the last 3 years, and I have swayed heavily into the ways of the world. I have never once denounced my faith, not will I ever, but I have made some pretty big mistakes. You have to give your all to living a Godly life and I haven't done that. My daughter is over a year old and this past Sunday was the first time she has been to Sunday morning Church Service. I don't pray as often as I should, I don't indulge myself into the Bible as much as I should, and I definitely don't obey God's word like I should either. Do I deserve to have a seat in heaven on the day of the rapture? Right now I believe the answer to that question is no. I know the truth and I believe in the truth and I want to live by the truth and I don't. Someone else deserves my spot right now. Are there things in my life that I should change, yes, and will I change them, yes because getting into heaven is my number one goal in life. My life is in shambles right now and I am working on picking up the pieces and God is on my side working on it right along with me. There will come a point in the near future that if you were to ask me this question again, I would probably be able to pick someone else but right now I can't do that. My letter would say something to the effect of this:

Michelle,

You know the life style that God wanted you to live and you chose to sway from it. When things got difficult for you, you always relied on God to fix the problem but you never served Him the way that the Bible declares you to do. You opened up your heart to the truth and you turned a way from it. God is a forgiving God, He loves you always and yet you still chose to ignore Him. Now that you have been left behind, things are going to be that much more difficult for you. The times ahead are going to be filled with torture and pain and you won't have the Holy Spirit to help guide you through it like you have your whole life. You called on God in your most difficult moments in life. You cried out to Him and begged Him to help you. He was there for you, He's never forsaken you, and He never turned His back on you. Just because you aren't living in the new earth that has been promised to you doesn't mean that you can't someday enjoy the pleasures that only He can give, but now, it is going to take so much more then He was asking from you in the beginning. God is a merciful God and you should know that. After everything you have been through, the only consistent thing in your life was Him. When your daughter died, you cried out to Him, but you never fully embraced all that He had to offer. When your trials and suffering came along, you said that the only reason why you were still standing was because you had Him in your life, but you never lived up to the Christian life style. When your husband was imprisoned you gave your life over to Him but you didn't sway from your way of life, you still were corrupted by the things that this world had to offer. "My God shall supply all my needs." That was a promise that He gave to you and you never asked for Him to help you, to provide for you, and yet when you needed help the most, He was there for you. Not you're friends, or your family; but He, God, was there for you. You never listened to His voice when He was calling out to you. You ignored all that He had to say because you were too busy with your own life to worry about what Christ wanted from you. You always said that "I can do all things through Christ who strengthens me," but you never fully gave it over to Him. You always held on to some of the pain instead of surrendering it to the one man who could provide you with the strength and that man was and is Jesus Christ. So now, we pray for you. You can get through this because you have God on your side. Never give up, you are some of the believers who were left behind so now it is up to you to move mountains and move them in the name of Christ. Give it all to Him, He died on that cross to bear your pain, your suffering, and with Him, you WILL be made whole again, never give up because ask yourself, is this something Jesus would do?" No, he wouldn't and if He had to, He would die all over again to make sure that people like you have, one day, a place in heaven to call home. Jesus loves you and always will no matter what the situation may be.

Sincerely,
Me

Wow, I never really realized how powerful a question like that could be. It really makes you realize how much you need to work on. God is good and He loves me and He will never leave me nor forsake me and I really need to give Him that same respect back. He has been here for me always and I need to learn how to give it completely to Him. I can't hold back anymore because it's because of Him that I am able to be so strong at times and so weak at others. I need to trust that all things happen in love. God knew what He was doing when He took my family away from me, now; I just need to listen to Him so I can find out why.

Letter 3:

Dear Loved Ones and Friends,

I know you are scared right now and maybe even angry. The trumpet has sounded and God has taken us to heaven. If only I could tell you everything will be ok and I will see you someday, but that is all up to you now. I am sorry for not being a better example to you, and for not praying for you everyday. I did pray but I feel like it wasn't enough and I let you down.

The days are going to be darker then ever before, but one thing still remains true. Jesus still died for you and if you want to you can accept him into your heart today and hopefully keep your faith and not deny him in the events to come. There is no easy way to say this but there will be no hope anywhere you will have to lean on the bible for hope. God didn't want it to be this way; his will was for all to believe. The funny thing is even with this devastating time that is approaching people are still going to deny Jesus. Even if some saw Him face to face at this very moment they would laugh and mock Him. I don't know if you will make it through with out giving up. I can only ask you to please, please remember who Jesus is, what he has done for you, what those who are gone told you about Him, how much He loves you.

I don't know what to say right now, but I love you and I believe in you and I do want to see you someday. I wanted you to find the truth so you wouldn't have to go through the tribulation. I can't even imagine what it must be like standing in your shoes right now. As I am writing this before the rapture takes place there have been many times I would have like to take the hurt for people but realized that I can't. I wanted to take people burdens but realized I was trying to pull one way and they were going the other way. Only God can take those burdens. Who am I?

My heart is sad today as I am writing this letter, I don't know who will find it because I am hoping everyone I know and care for are with me. God says there will be no tears in heaven but right now there are tears falling on my desk. Who am I, out of everyone else that deserves God's grace and mercy, and I am not perfect and have struggled a lot in my days. But I do know who Jesus is and so can you. If you will just say this prayer; *"Dear Lord Jesus, I know I am a sinner, please forgive me and come into my life as my Lord and Savoir"*. He will forgive you of your sins. That was the easy part though I am afraid, now to go through without denying Him will be the challenge.

No one can tell you how chaotic this world will be soon, the bible says that this time will be like nothing ever seen before. We have already seen horror after horror. No matter what happens please hold onto the knowledge that Jesus Christ died to save your soul and that He loves you more than anyone else in the world. Even if you have to die one day because you will not deny Him, it will be worth it, because you will be with Him for eternity.

I hope you realize how much you are loved and how precious you are to those that are gone now and to the Lord. If you are reading this, maybe you can

30

make the difference of heaven or hell in someone else's life around you. You are not alone, there will be others out there that find the truth of Jesus Christ and will not deny Him no matter what. Keep going, keep pressing on, ask God to help you each and everyday, read Revelation in the bible to see what is in store for you, so you will be ready to face it and stand courageously, knowing that you are a child of God and one day you will be with Jesus.

I love you and believe in you. You can make it, it just won't be easy.

Love,

Liz

Letter 4:

This is for you (me)

Loved ones, friends, and others have vanished. Jesus came just as he promised and has taken unto Him the ones who were watching and ready. Stop blaming God! You made your choices, but you need to know that God still loves you! For God so loved the world that he gave his one and only son that anyone who believes in Him should not perish, but have everlasting life (John 3:16). It's not God's will for any to perish, but that all people repent and accept Jesus as Lord and Savior. God is giving you this moment to make your peace with him. Accept Jesus Christ, the one who died for you and paid the price of your sins with his blood. Don't pass up this moment; you might not get another chance. You could die in the next moment. If you die without accepting Jesus, in that moment you'll have made your final choice. Pray:

God forgive me, I've sinned against you. I'm lost and I need you. Jesus I give my life to you. Thank you for dying for me and paying the price for my sins, and making the way so I could come to God. Be Lord over my life from this moment and

forever. I need you and accept you as my Savior. God, I thank you for giving me this
moment. Amen.

Terrible things are happening and things are going to get worse. There will
be a person who talks about peace, love and world unity. Don't trust him.
He'll seem godly but he's evil. He'll want everyone to take a mark (his mark)
on their forehead or right hand. No matter what do not take this mark! If
you do, at that moment you've made your final choice, rejecting Jesus Christ.
There's only two choices, and that's all there's ever been. Each one of us will
come to this moment, and make our final choice:

1. Accept Jesus Christ as Savior and Lord, spend eternity with him in his
    love, peace and joy.
2. Reject Jesus Christ- spend eternity apart from him in the Lake of Fire,
    all the time knowing that you didn't have to come to this place of
    torment. Jesus died and shed his blood and paid this price for you.

From,

One who chose and accepted Jesus Christ as Savior and Lord